How Psychics and Mediums Work, The Spirit and the Aura

How Psychics and Mediums Work, The Spirit and the Aura

James McQuitty

A James McQuitty Book

First Published 2014

This Edition August 2020

This book contains some updated chapters from the author's 2004 book: Over the Rainbow

Many other books in both paperback and kindle formats by James McQuitty are for sale worldwide through Amazon

Other titles include:

Adventures in Time and Space

Christianity: The Sad and Shameful Truth

Escape From Hell

Golden Enlightenment – Twenty Year Anniversary Edition

Immortality

Know Thyself, Be Thyself

Spiritual Astro-Numerology: The Complete Guide

The Evolvement of the Soul

The Reason Why You Were Born

The Spirit World Realms

The Wisdom Oracle: An Aid to Accessing Your Inner or Higher Self Wisdom

Find the Author at Facebook:

https://www.facebook.com/mcquittybooks

https://www.facebook.com/jamesmcquittysharing

Table of Contents

Introduction 7

1. How Psychics Work 12
2. How Mediums Work... 18
3. From Psychic to Medium 22
4. What we should expect from a psychic 35
5. What we should expect from a medium 39
6. The difficulties mediums encounter and why predictions can fail 43
7. Mediumship: Has Many Expressions 50
8. The Spirit and the Aura.. 60

Conclusion 76

Websites 81
Recommended Reading 84

About the Author... 87

Introduction

This book will help readers to understand how psychics and mediums work.

It will also help them to understand more about the human spirit and the energies which surround each of us, often referred to as the "aura".

As for me, it has been many years since 1981 when I first began to earnestly research the spiritual realities of life. During this time I have attended hundreds of demonstrations of varying forms of mediumship, and sat in numerous development circles. I have also read countless books on spirit philosophy and others dealing with scientific research.

During this time I have learnt and discovered much. This has given my life far greater meaning and purpose than I could ever have imagined.

My advice to every reader is to embrace as much genuine spiritual knowledge as they possibly can.

When we recognise that life is eternal, and its implications, it most certainly can help us to cope far better with the challenges that physical life presents us with.

We can then recognise and accept that no 'death' represents a permanent loss or separation. We understand that, sooner or later, we all journey onwards to our true home in spirit life, and meet again with those we care about or love.

My earthly 'mission', as I could call it, since I know it is part of my soul plan for this lifetime, has been to share what I have been privileged to learn through my writing.

Naturally, I feel confident in stating that what I am sharing with readers in this book is genuine factual information. Or at very least a good interpretation of it!

However, I do recognise the fact that over the course of time one's truth, or interpretation of it, can develop. It can expand or grow or even find alternative ways in which it can be presented, viewed or expressed.

Indeed, I have noticed that different spirit guides and

teachers, just like many writers upon Earth, at times find different or alternative ways of saying what can, quite often, amount to the same thing! Terms used can and often do vary greatly.

"Semantics", as the lovely guide "White Feather", who speaks through the trance medium Robert Goodwin, has so often said.

So worry not, my dear reader, if I term something in a slightly different way to some other writer. Even if they insist their way is the right way; for in due course of time it will not matter, we shall find ourselves "home" in spirit life and understand all these things thoroughly, and may again describe them in a completely different way to how we have done upon Earth!

Readers may also find that one spirit communicator says something which is contrary to what another one says. How can this be? Most new seekers will wonder. And while some of what I am saying in this introduction may not seem entirely relevant to how psychics and mediums work, or to the spirit and the aura, it is in a sense relative. As I will explain.

First though, why does one spirit communicator say one thing and another something that seemingly or clearly contradicts what the first communicator has said? The answer to this is quite simple.

The answer is because in spirit life not everyone there has reached the same level of awareness and progression. There are countless different realms or spheres. The wiser we become, the higher or more progressed is the realm we will inhabit.

Those in higher realms have far greater knowledge and understanding than those in less progressed realms. They generally have a broader and more elevated level of awareness and may know things that those in realms below are yet to discover. Just as we tend to gradually learn and understand more as we progress through life from childhood to become adults who learn so much through life experiences!

So we find that different spirit communicators can be speaking from different states of progression and understanding; from advanced or less advanced levels.

As it is with spirit communicators, upon Earth one psychic may work to a different level of capability and understanding to another. And one medium may be more advanced and capable than another.

I hope readers have enjoyed my little introduction to this book; it may, perhaps, help them to understand a few things they previously did not. I hope also that it encourages them to look forward to discovering more, and initially, how psychics and mediums work, which follows immediately in the first two chapters.

1. How Psychics Work

People who are genuinely psychic have a heightened sensitivity. Consciously or unconsciously they open their auric senses (I say more on the aura later) and receive vibrational information.

Some psychics, and particularly those more 'professional', may embrace "psychometry". This involves handling something belonging to another person in order to glean information from it. Although any sensitive person may at times, and quite naturally and inadvertently, receive impressions from an object, or indeed from the atmosphere in a room, and especially so if something emotionally charged occurred there.

However, in relation to psychometry, every object, in fact all matter, can be imprinted with vibrations; and particularly those worn or handled frequently.

Although most people who practice psychometry say they prefer an object that is metallic, such as a ring, necklace, bracelet or wristwatch. These are considered to 'register' (or absorb) a stronger vibration – making the vibrations (theoretically at least) easier to 'read' (decode or decipher). Just as a stronger TV or radio signal produces a better and clearer picture or sound.

The observant reader may perhaps realise that since it is the energy of the person (imprinted on the object) that is actually being 'read', an object is not strictly necessary. Indeed, many psychics – knowingly or unknowingly – can "pick-up" on the vibrations of another without any form of physical touch. In much the same way as when any of us may sense when someone is approaching us from behind.

Psychic sense, which to degree we all have, since we are all spirit beings, is equally capable of acknowledging when someone is staring at us from a moderate distance (across a room etc.).

What allows us to sense someone in these two examples is our own aura (personal energy field). Firstly, the aura can be larger and more sensitive than one might imagine. So when someone approaches us from behind his or her energy touches our energy, and we sense that they are there. Across a room, or even across a street, someone staring will "project energy", most generally without realising that they are doing so. If projected sufficiently, again this will touch our own energy field and alert us. As I have said, we are all capable of receiving and projecting energy, and without realising do so regularly. (In fact, almost constantly when awake).

Someone who is purely psychic (without mediumistic ability) cannot give anyone a message from someone in the spiritual realms (physically deceased).

However, if their psychic ability is well developed they may be capable of reading much about us from our energy vibrations, whether utilising psychometry or simply by concentrating upon us (again, this will cause their energy to temporarily link with our energy).

Distance does not prevent or even hinder such an energy link! Which is why an accomplished psychic can be somewhere far away and still link with our energy. Sometimes, particularly for a postal reading, a psychic might ask for a photograph or a lock of hair etc., the photograph will act for them as a focal point for concentration, while a lock of hair, having registered our vibrations, will assist them to "attune" to us.

To anyone new to such investigations this may sound far-fetched, but it is nonetheless perfectly true. It is the reason why secret service agencies around the world have often utilised the abilities of psychics. At the top end of the scale of ability a highly proficient psychic will be able to "tune-in" to the recent thoughts and activities of our life. For example, they may learn what we have been thinking about and doing, whom we have met, and what we might have discussed, and much more. If they have a particular question about us an answer may even present itself to them. Therefore a top-notch psychic, and I am not suggesting that many, if any, reach a standard where all and any sought information will be forthcoming to them, can be most receptive and glean much information from someone's energy field.

How much is stored in our energy? Well, quite literally, everything. All thoughts and emotions to actions and ideas, there are no secrets to our energy field - everything about us is there.

Strong impressions, those that make deep impressions in our life, and especially those more recent, are particularly forthcoming and more readily accessible to a psychic.

This is why strong emotional impressions of love, rejection, joy and pain, are so often "picked up" by a psychic. It is similar to what I said earlier for psychometry – an object regularly worn will absorb a stronger impression. Likewise, a stronger and intensely felt emotion or reaction will send a stronger signal into one's own energy field.

It must register there because our energy field "is us". It is part of our essence as a spirit being. We cannot "escape ourselves". All in our life is registered within our soul totality. Consciously we may forget, but nothing, even of the slightest relevance, is ever totally lost.

We are all spirit beings temporarily functioning through a physical body and we each have our own aura – which effectively is our spirit or soul upon Earth. Each of us is capable of using our spiritual faculties to the degree that we have progressed. As in all endeavours of life practise will improve. A would be artist who wishes to paint a landscape will not find it very easy when they first try. But if they have such ability within them, gradually, perhaps with help, guidance, training and practise they will reveal their ability.

In such a scenario we would not expect all to produce landscapes of the same quality. In other words some will find that they have greater aptitude or ability than others.

Psychic ability (and mediumship) is likewise no different; some will find within themselves a finer aptitude than others.

2. How Mediums Work

A genuine medium - that is someone who is clairvoyant, clairaudient or clairsentient, or can use a mixture of all three, is a go between, a link, and a translator of telepathic transmissions from those who reside in the spirit realms. Such mediums are termed "mental mediums" because what they receive comes through the faculty of mind.

The word "clairvoyance" translates to mean "clear seeing". It is the most commonly used term to refer to a medium. A spirit person will send telepathic images to a medium in the hope that firstly, they will see them clearly as an impression upon their "mind's eye" (the faculty that allows us to see in dreams when we sleep), and that secondly they will be able to 'translate' or gather a meaning from what they receive.

As can be realised, we are already asking much.

The word "clairaudience" translates to mean "clear hearing". Some mediums are better able to receive telepathic thought transmissions, rather than or in addition to images. So naturally, if this is the case, a spirit person will transmit their thoughts and hope that these, via the subconscious mind of the medium, will register and instantly be relayed to the conscious thoughts of the medium.

Again we are asking much, for the medium has to isolate their own thoughts from those they receive. Although some, being blessed with a degree of physical mediumship qualities, are able to have the incoming thoughts enhanced by means of ectoplasm (a spirit substance obtained from the medium) so that they may hear the spirit communicator's voice in a similar way to how we hear physical voices.

The word "clairsentience" translates to mean "clear feeling". Many mediums work in this way in addition to either or both clairvoyance and clairaudience. There are also some mediums who solely receive communications in this way.

If the spirit person knows that a medium is better at receiving in this fashion, rather than telepathically transmitting images or thoughts, they will send feelings.

A medium who is accomplished at receiving and interpreting in this way can still be most accurate in what they pass as a message. Much, as could be expected, will depend upon how well developed the medium is, and how intuitively receptive they are at understanding the message behind or contained within the feelings.

The method of spirit transmission in image, thought, or feeling, as I have said, can reflect the receptivity of the medium. However, it is also possible that the spirit communicators themselves will favour a particular method of transmission.

The personality does not immediately change upon passing. Therefore, one who was good at verbal communication may prefer to telepathically 'speak' their thoughts. While some, because they may find it more difficult to telepathically picture or phrase their thoughts, may prefer sending feelings. (Animals too, can transmit thoughts and feelings).

It should also be borne in mind that there is no instant understanding gained upon passing, all needs to be learned, and it is not necessarily easy to telepathically send thoughts, even if the person was a good conversationalist when upon Earth.

3. From Psychic to Medium

A medium can be utilising psychic ability, along with mediumship. It is often difficult to be sure how much of each is actually being used.

Since we are all spirit beings, we each have the potential to use and develop further any natural psychic or mediumistic capabilities. Many will deny any such capability and say that they have no psychic ability, let alone any mediumistic ability. Yet it is commonplace to experience my earlier example of "knowing" when someone is approaching from behind, or staring at us, which are both displays of psychic intuitiveness.

The following is an outline, a rough guide, to a range of psychic through to mediumistic abilities from minor psychic to the heights of mediumship. Each level embraces those below.

Purely Psychic

Level 1 - As previously mentioned, without seeing or hearing, it is sensed when someone is approaching. When being stared at we will "feel" this and turn to face the person who is looking at us.

Level 2 - We sense when the telephone is about to ring, and may instinctively know who will be calling and perhaps why. We suddenly think of someone, often a person we have not seen for some time, and either they telephone, visit, we meet them on the street, or hear some news about them.

Level 3 - Those at this level may be aware that they have some ability more than the average person, although they may choose to tell only family and close friends. They will, for example, be able to read the tealeaves or some other tool, even if in a limited way. Or similarly they will occasionally use Playing, Tarot or other cards.

Level 4 - Next are those who more readily admit to their ability with one or other of the aforementioned tools, and are more inclined to use them. So they may take great delight in giving mini readings for anyone who is interested. In addition or alternative to the tools listed, they may embrace psychometry.

Level 5 - We now reach the level when some of those with sufficient psychic ability may decide that they can use this to earn a little money. How much, depends upon their confidence, desire, needs and conscience.

At this level a prop will most certainly be used, whether a crystal ball or more commonly Tarot or similar cards, Rune stones, or one of many other choices utilised around the world. A reading from someone at this level may be a bit of a hit or miss affair, for each day the ability they have to attune to our energies can fluctuate. Also, their energies may or may not be capable of *finely* attuning to our energies, although in most cases they will have some success.

Level 6 - Again, this level will embrace such as the Tarot card reader. But, at the top end of the purely psychic scale, some are more proficient, and more in control of their ability. They are therefore more capable of attuning to the energies of a range of sitters. Experience will naturally assist their ability to provide an accurate reading; for this will have taught them how to interpret what they are able to receive; those adept at interpreting can be proven most accurate. While a genuine willingness to be of service does make a difference, for those of a sympathetic nature are more likely to achieve a finer vibratory link.

A Mixture of Psychic and Mediumship

Level 7 - At this level we begin the overlap between psychic ability and mediumship. Many at this level will be offering their services to the public, but will most likely call themselves a psychic or a clairvoyant psychic. A sitting with someone at this level of development will provide all the information obtained by a proficient psychic along with a little input from perhaps one or two close relatives from the spirit realms. As a gauge let us say that the reading will be 90% psychic and 10% mediumistic.

Level 8 - To gauge in absolute terms we could have a level for every percentage point and then some, so from hereon it can be assumed that there are many levels (or sub levels) between each one that I have listed.

For the sake of simplicity, let us say that those at this level use 75% psychic ability and 25% mediumistic ability. In addition to psychically obtained information they may achieve a tentative link with relatives who might give a few family names that we recognise, along with their love. Any other information may well lack clarity, and we may find that they have to ask a number of questions, which will hopefully enable us to understand the communication. This may happen if the input that they are receiving is unclear or perhaps symbolic, and therefore very difficult for them to interpret.

Level 9 - Let us now jump straight to the middle ground. To someone who may simply call him or herself a medium or clairvoyant, but who still utilises 50% psychic intuitiveness or receptivity along with 50% mediumship. Here we can get a very accurate psychic reading, but the mediumship, albeit better than someone at the level below, may still lack clarity. They may get a number of names that are recognisable, but they may also get many that are not. They may pass a reasonably accurate description of a close relative or friend, although it may lack some element of precision, perhaps it will be most accurate apart from one detail. Such a sitting would be satisfactory to a point, but would most likely leave us unsure as to whether a link was truly made, or whether guesswork was involved.

Level 10 - From the level below to this and beyond we will find a vast number of psychics and mediums with receptivity that is variable between mediocre to highly accurate. Although we are now nearing the level of more dedicated mediumship, those at this level will still use psychic intuitiveness but typically this will account for only say 25% of their reading, while 75% will involve mediumship (although not necessarily of outstanding accomplishment). They will almost certainly call themselves a medium, or if being more descriptive may choose to use the title clairvoyant, clairaudient, or clairsentient, perhaps with medium tagged on at the end. Here any reading may start with a little psychically gleaned information, to help get the mediumship attuned, but will (hopefully) quickly develop to pass information obtained from at least one, sometimes several, spirit communicators.

Pure Mediumship

Level 11 - Although many mediums use their psychic abilities to get them attuned or as a starting link, those whom we can put towards the top of our list really do attempt to use mediumship at all private sittings (or public demonstrations). They will normally call themselves a medium, but once again the accuracy of the spirit communications they receive can vary greatly.

At the lower level of pure mediumship, it is possible that only 30% of what they receive will be readily understood and accepted by the recipient. A good percentage of what they attempt to relay would be found vague, for two reasons. One, is because the medium is not fully attuned to the spirit communicator, so the incoming telepathic message is difficult for them to receive with any precision. The second reason, is because even if the message is well received, it is still a telepathic thought transmission, often in symbolic imagery, so the spirit communicator relies upon the medium to be sufficiently aware or intuitive to act as interpreter. If the medium misunderstands a symbolic communication things can become most confusing. If both reasons are a problem, then we really will struggle to make sense of what the spirit communicator is attempting to say.

Level 12 - As we move up the mediumship levels the successful reception and onward communication to the sitter improves in quality or accuracy. Let us introduce a variable and say that at this level the "success" rate reaches 60-70% (there are many mediums who are somewhere between each level, and perhaps especially so between levels 11 and 12). We will call "success" a communication that is readily accepted as accurate. At this level success reaches a standard that I think we can quite fairly call good-to-very good mediumship. (Not that one wishes to act as judge).

Level 13+ - Hereon, mediumship that achieves a success rate of 75% and above can be deemed excellent. The top end of this scale (80%-100%) is achieved by very few mediums. All those who develop mediumship are ambassadors of spirit, for attempting to demonstrate proof of eternal life, we should be proud of them.

Often it has taken courage; and always it demands personal commitment, perseverance, and in the vast majority of cases a willingness to sacrifice. This can include aspects of their personal life due to the amount of time given for travelling and demonstrating, as well as financially. Contrary to what some believe, the majority, particularly those who serve the spiritualist community, receive remuneration that is the equivalent of far less than the minimum wage, if anything at all, for some merely ask for travel expenses.

As I said earlier, my "levels" are of course rough guides. As may be gathered, not only are there many ranges of ability (levels) into which we could attempt to pigeonhole psychics and mediums, but that even these will have many variables. For instance, a psychic-medium may believe that what they are relaying is a high percentage of information from spirit communicators, when in fact they may inadvertently be picking up information psychically.

Another important variable that should be noted by all that attend for private readings, or public demonstrations, is that the atmosphere generated by individual or group can and does have an impact upon the receptivity of the medium.

A medium is effectively a receiving station, one capable of attunement with higher frequencies of vibration. Just like a TV or radio, if their attunement is not fine their reception is poor or non-existent.

Mediums are not mechanical. Their receptive attunement is associated with their aura through which the telepathic imagery, thoughts and/or feelings pass. These fields of energy are not isolated from sitters or the world at large. Their energy fields, indeed our own energy fields too, are constantly being bombarded with vibrations from many sources. Not from the spiritual dimensions alone, but also from the physical world. Much of this we are largely immune to, for it is mostly familiar to our energy vibrations. But when a medium prepares to demonstrate and link with those from the spirit side of life, their sensitivity and vibrations are heightened, and so naturally they become more aware of thoughts and feelings. This is as it should be to receive input from those in spirit. However, it also makes them more vulnerable to the thoughts, feelings and emotions of the sitter(s).

In this state of "heightened awareness" if one or more of the sitters are of a hostile nature they can quite easily interfere with communication. This is because such an attitude creates its own adverse frequency. To the medium it is like trying to align an aerial in a positive direction, while the sitter(s) in the very same air space align one in a negative direction. The result, as it would be with a TV or radio signal, is that it causes interference.

Therefore, when a sitter attends with a negative attitude that says, "Prove it to me", or, "I know this is a trick", or, "I don't believe but the wife dragged me along", they are literally sending out a vibrational energy signal that is counter-productive. This can make communication more difficult, and in consequence less precise or accurate.

To the medium the problems caused may amount to the same as trying to view a flickering screen, listen to a fragmented audio recording, or feel what a spirit person wished them to feel while also being bombarded by negative feelings by the sitter(s).

This is not to say that all less perfect sittings are down to the sitter(s), for mediums, just like all of us, can have off days. They may be physically tired, or under mentally or emotionally stress in their personal life, so their batteries may be weakened, and as a result they may have difficulty concentrating and tuning in, which can make precise reception more difficult.

However, on the positive side, from personal experience, I can say that if one gives mediumship a fair chance and always approach with an open mind, later if not sooner, they *will* find a medium capable of assuring them of life beyond the physical spectrum.

4. What we should expect from a psychic

As will have gathered from reading chapter one, someone who is purely psychic will glean all the information they might pass to someone at a sitting from the person's own energy field. To reiterate, none of this information will be from anyone resident in the spiritual realms, all will be from the sitter.

Whether they use an object, as with psychometry, or a crystal ball or tarot cards etc. will reflect their preferred method of attuning to their sitter's energies, and sensitising (using their own sensitivity to interpret) what they receive.

So what should we expect from a psychic? Well, typically they will tell us things we largely already know and can confirm as correct or accurate. For instance, they may start with aspects of our life that are more to the forefront of our thoughts and emotions. We may, for example, be considering a change of employment, home, or have other financial concerns which they will mention. Or relationship satisfaction, worry or problems might be forthcoming. These may of course be expanded upon in suitable detail that is personally applicable to us.

While any issues or concerns we may have in relation to family and friends might also be revealed. Even what we have learned from others will be registered within our own personal energy field.

What they may go on to perceive (as chapter one, dependent upon the sensitivity and ability of the psychic) may be more deeply held thoughts. Such as those that reveal our inner character - what sort of person we truly are, perhaps also any fears and phobias, and examples of things we may particularly enjoy or dislike.

Additionally, it is conceivable that things we may temporarily have forgotten may be mentioned. This is possible because the *greater self*, embraced or linked with our energy vibrations, will have stored everything with perceivable value of which we have experience. Our energies, or energy fields, are of spirit, and infallible, although in the fullness of time irrelevant memories may fade.

Bearing in mind what I have said one might say, "Why bother having a sitting with a psychic, if all they can tell me are things I already know".

Well, at the level of psychic perception so far mentioned, the sitting serves no purpose other than demonstrating that such psychic ability exists.

If we seek communication with someone residing in the spiritual realms this will not be forthcoming.

However, since we are dealing with variables, if the psychic is sensitive enough, useful guidance may also be forthcoming, even via a purely psychic link.

This is because our energy field, at a higher vibration in our being, itself contains spiritual knowledge pertaining to us. Once more we are dealing with the sensitivity and ability of each individual psychic. If they are able to glean information from our higher vibrations, which are often referred to as the "higher-mind" (or "higher-self"), then greater knowledge can, potentially, become known to them. As for the higher-mind, it is in possession of higher knowledge, such as our life plan or purpose. Furthermore, and straying slightly from the purely psychic, it is possible that thoughts and ideas (guidance) might filter into the thoughts of the psychic from another mind, albeit without the psychic being aware from whence the thoughts originate.

As I have said, a psychic with "top-notch" calibre, in my opinion, is rare. As my "levels" indicate, the finer the quality the more inclined to develop mediumship. However, it is also fair to say that not all psychics, no matter how good, have the potential to develop mediumistically. Their own pre-birth life-plan may lead them on a different pathway.

What we should expect from a psychic is therefore dependent upon their individual sensitivity and ability to interpret the vibrational information they receive. It is still largely their ability to translate, to make sense of what they receive, that will either satisfy, or frustrate, or mystify us.

5. What we should expect from a medium

The first thing we should expect to receive through a medium is "proof of survival" (continuity of life after the death of the physical body). Although, I must also say, that the "philosophy of spirit" imparted by some mediums at public meetings before their demonstration, is also of great importance.

In order to give evidence of "survival" a medium will seek to receive a telepathic link from whoever comes forward from the spirit realms to communicate with us (or the intended recipient at a public demonstration). This will be a freewill decision made by the spirit communicator, for it is always their choice whether to communicate; nobody can ever summon or "call them up", it simply does not work that way.

Spirit people are as free as we are to choose when and whom they visit, with vast numbers living in realms where they enjoy far greater freedom of expression than is available to many upon Earth.

More often the "spirit" (as people living in the spirit world tend to be called) will be a relative or loved one, otherwise a friend (or occasionally a spirit guide or helper). Whoever it is, in a typical sitting they will attempt to identify themselves. They may, if the medium is clairaudient, give their name, or identify themselves as Mother or Father etc.

If the medium is able to clairvoyantly see them, they will most likely do their best to describe them. While if the medium is purely clairsentient, the communicator will most likely try to impart to them the 'feeling' of their relationship to us.

The communicator may also mention some habits or hobbies they had while upon Earth. Or they may share some memories they have, and hopefully those which we will be able to confirm.

Having established that we recognise the communicator, before they end their communication they may say if they have any particular reason, other than proving their presence, for making the link.

This can simply be to reassure us that they are fine, that they still love us, and to show us that they are still taking an interest in our life and well-being.

If it is to offer us some guidance, it is important to remember that this is *only* their opinion. They naturally may wish to help us, but we should only take notice if we are in agreement with what is communicated. In the same was as we might have done when they were in physical form. We should bear in mind that 'death' does not transform anyone into a guru of wisdom. Upon passing the majority for some considerable time remain very much as they were when upon Earth.

There are a couple of things a genuine medium should not do. Firstly, they should not expect us to answer any questions other than to reply yes, no, or that we don't know. Secondly, they should not claim any kind of infallibility. Furthermore, if one considers their fee excessive I would suggest not to book an appointment with them.

If anyone needs help looking for a genuine medium they may seek assistance from a number of Spiritist and spiritualist organisations such as included on my Websites section; or of course find a trustworthy word of mouth recommendation.

6. The difficulties mediums encounter and why predictions can fail

---

When one thinks of the different "levels" of mediumship I have already covered, I am sure that any reasonable person would be quite surprised to find a medium who did not on at least some occasions encounter difficulties.

Even the better exponents of mediumship are, like all of us, prone to "off days". So it would be surprising to find any that on occasions did not have problems with their reception, and by consequence at least here and there "get things wrong" or make mistakes. The lower their level, the more so; and I mean no disrespect when I say so. We should always remember that mediums are literally attempting to communicate with people who are living in a different dimension of eternal life.

It is to their credit that so many mediums are able to receive and interpret as well as they do. So with this in mind let me summarise and expand upon the difficulties they encounter, and why predictions can fail.

Firstly, to reiterate, we must consider the different levels of mediumship, for these do vary considerably. Some mediums are more naturally sensitive, and many have been psychic or mediumistic from childhood. While others begin to recognise their potential as adults, and from whatever age this happens, gradually develop their sensitivity; and by practise, patience and perseverance, usually through development circles with meditation, enhance their receptivity and learn to interpret the communications they receive.

Even then, if every potential medium were to put all of their spare time into enhancing their sensitivity and learning how best to interpret the often symbolic telepathic communications they receive, quite naturally, some would still be more finely attuned than others.

Symbolic imagery I understand is used by spirit communicators to mediums because of the difficulty of long-drawn messages (it is easier to send the thought of an image than a full sentence). It should also be recognised that thought communications are used quite naturally in the spirit realms between the people there, and there thoughts also convey a fuller meaning.

These days few mediums reach the level of sensitive receptivity required to receive surnames and postal addresses on a regular basis. This is perhaps because there are now just too many distractions put in front of us. Whereas in days prior to TV, computers and mobile phones, and going back still further, to before radio, when there were fewer distractions, by all accounts there were more mediums of the calibre to communicate surnames and postal addresses.

The development of mediumship is rarely achieved without great effort and commitment. No more than it is easy to become a top-level artist, singer, or for that matter furniture maker. I can saw a piece of wood in two but this does not make me a carpenter. I can change a light bulb and an electrical plug but this does not make me an electrician. Very few in this present age are willing to devote their time to a long drawn-out occupational apprenticeship, let alone to one as precarious, and generally with little financial reward, as mediumship.

Some people are natural born mediums; but many others hope to develop their abilities by taking courses. However, people should recognise that no one can develop mediumship without the assistance and cooperation of their guides in spirit life. It is not in the life-plan of some who may be left disappointed; but of course there is no harm trying if one feels drawn to doing so. I could take an art class but I strongly doubt that I would become another Vincent van Gogh or Leonardo da Vinci.

Why do predictions from those in the spiritual realms fail?

Firstly, we must remember that relatives who communicate are often on an elementary level of the astral world. At this level, which we are told is a near replica to the Earth-plane they often know little if any more than the person to whom they are passing a message. Therefore, any prediction, or what a medium perceives as a prediction, is often meaningless.

What can happen is that the relative or friend merely wants to show us that they have been taking an interest in what is happening in our day-to-day life. Or they may wish to make a suggestion, or pass advice as they might have done when upon Earth. They may even be privy to certain events in our life that may appear to be leading to a certain conclusion, and they may say so, either as a misguided prediction or perhaps, and I would like to think more generally, as a forecast of a likely outcome.

However, via *some* mediums (not all), this may come across as a "sure" prediction. Once again we are dealing with the level, attunement and experience of the medium, and as explained, this can vary greatly.

The medium relaying the message may be under the impression that the prediction is a certainty. Mediums in general have to learn to trust what they receive, to know the difference between a spirit communication and their own imagination, and sometimes this trust may inadvertently encourage them to suggest that such and such a prediction will come to fruition.

Therefore, either because the medium has misunderstood, or indeed because of the communicators desire to believe that what they "foresee" will occur, the message is passed as a sure prediction. But, what the recipient should be receiving is often no more than the opinion of the friend or relative.

Higher guides, our real guides, are far less likely to offer predictions. Especially concerning our physical day-to-day life, for they have total respect for our freewill. So without good reason they will rarely make predictions, for by the very nature of the word, a prediction is most generally a "guess".

Although if we have concerns and ask for guidance, particularly of a spiritual nature, a guide may offer their thoughts or an opinion, but they will leave us to make our own decisions.

Personally, I would not blame an over-zealous spirit

relative for trying to give information, whether misunderstood by the medium or wrongly anticipated by themselves. I am sure that they and the mediums endeavour to do their best, but like us, are only human (even if in spirit life). So errors are bound to occur, just as they do upon the Earth-plane, and we, when we receive a message, can also be guilty of misunderstanding or jumping to wrong conclusions.

The bottom line is that life on Earth is our own to live!!

7. Mediumship: Has Many Expressions

In addition to the 'gifts' or abilities that come under the banner of "mental mediumship", there are many other expressions of mediumship. They include trance, physical, psychic-spiritual art, and healing mediumship.

The following is an outline of each.

Trance Mediumship

Trance mediumship, in a sense, is a more direct form of communication because a spirit person, who is usually a guide, although occasionally a relative or friend, is effectively able to speak directly through the entranced medium to everyone present.

At least this is so at a deep level of trance, when the consciousness of the medium is sufficiently withdrawn from their physical body to ensure that they are unaware of what is being said by the spirit communicator, and therefore unlikely to interfere to any tangible degree.

There are also "lesser" states of trance, such as "overshadowing" when a spirit communicator may inspire a medium to relay their thoughts, for instance, at a gathering of people during a spiritualist demonstration or service.

At its best deep trance can be wonderful to witness. Excellent communication is possible in this way, and many wonderful books have been produced. Examples include the teachings of Silver Birch, of White Feather, Red Cloud and White Eagle.

Some mediums work in a lesser depth of trance and their consciousness may remain close enough to their physical body to hear what is said through them by the spirit communicator. In this lesser depth of trance what the spirit guide may wish to say can still come through the medium, but is more susceptible to interference from the thoughts of the medium. Therefore making it less reliable and prone to possible influence by the thoughts, beliefs and opinions of the medium.

Physical Mediumship

Physical mediumship can take many forms. The wonderful thing about it, as the name implies, is that it can be witnessed with physical senses. Unfortunately, development is often undertaken in total darkness - because light can be harmful to the medium and make phenomena more difficult to develop.

In an ideal scenario though, when sufficient energies have been built, and this can take many sittings and sometimes many years too, a red light can be introduced to enable vision.

On occasions those lucky enough to witness a top demonstration find that a friend or relative will actually materialise in physical form, so that they can see, hear, and converse with them, and with permission even touch them.

Regrettably, very few are lucky enough to find themselves in the position to sit in such a demonstration – more generally called a "physical circle". This is because such circles are nearly always "closed shops". The reason for this is because of the delicate nature of blending energies. This is entirely undertaken from the spirit side of life, but they are reliant upon having suitable sitters present – those who will generate a harmonious atmosphere.

Direct voice, as were produced through the wonderful Leslie Flint sittings (see Websites), is perhaps the next best form of communication to materialisation. This is when a spirit person effectively speaks direct to those present, with their thoughts passing through to a spirit constructed voice box or physical trumpet where it transforms to audible sound waves.

This may sound technical, and from the spirit side of life it undoubtedly is, but at the physical level what can be received is a voice that often is very much a perfect replica of the communicator's voice when upon Earth. Once all is in place conversation is as instantaneous as upon Earth, for thought travels faster than the speed of light.

Other examples of physical phenomena include levitation, apports (the materialisation of objects), spirit lights appearing and 'dancing' around, tables or objects being moved by unseen spirit people, and much more.

I regard physical mediumship as the "ultimate proof". It cannot be demonstrated to everyone, because of the need for a harmonious atmosphere. Those with a hostile "it is all a trick" mentality are least likely to witness, because the negative energies they project would certainly be counterproductive. On the other hand, an enquirer who is undecided, with neutral energies and an open mind, would be welcomed.

Psychic or Spiritual Art

Psychic art - as more traditionally called, or Spiritual art as perhaps more befitting, is most commonly the portrait drawing (or painting) of spirit people (or animals). The portraits can be of known relatives or friends, and recognisable to the recipient.

Occasionally, other spirit friends are drawn, guides or helpers for instance. Although the drawing of such personalities may not represent proof of survival, they can be pleasing and reassuring to receive, especially by someone seeking to work more closely with their spirit guides or helpers. A name or description may also be confirmed by a completely different medium.

Such inspired artists can work in different ways. Some are capable artists in their own right and are able to draw the portrait of the spirit person they clairvoyantly see. While others have no obvious artistic ability and find themselves either guided by unseen hand or during the process inspired or overshadowed as in the early stages of trance.

In whichever way inspired, the numbers of drawings with photographic evidence of accuracy later produced by numerous (thousands) of recipients is undeniable by all but the most closed-minded sceptic. One book above all others I would recommend to those interested is: *Faces of the Living Dead*, with the artwork of Frank Leah, put together by Paul Miller.

Healing Mediumship

Healing energies can flow through those mediums inspired to work in this field. The flow of energy is often described as, "from spirit, through spirit, to spirit". Which means the energies that flow from the spiritual dimensions in response to prayerful request (from spirit), pass through the aura of the healer (through spirit), to the aura of the recipient (to spirit). This is often achieved with "hands-on" contact of healer to patient.

Spiritual healing energies are intended to re-harmonise or restore balance to the aura (or finer energy bodies), and to the chakras, and as necessary and whenever possible by natural resonance to the physical body. Many factors will determine whether or not a recipient benefits from spiritual healing. Diet and general bodily maintenance naturally play a part. It is also important that any underlying cause of disharmony is reduced and better still eliminated. Often, a 'patient' will need to examine the way in which they think and consequently act. This is because the mind and emotions often play a part in disrupting auric energies.

Healing can also flow any distance in response to healing prayers. The healer does not require the presence of the recipient; indeed they can be on opposite sides of the globe.

The power of thought is more powerful than most people realise, and healing prayers are effectively an altruistic positive thought. Therefore, whenever anyone (particularly an accomplished healer) prays for healing, the thought acts as a carrier wave. Spirit helpers often assist this, effectively boosting the vibrational signal. They do so in order to ensure that it reaches its intended recipient. The thought signal and the energies that it brings endeavour to re-harmonise the recipients' auric field.

Some people respond better to distant (or absent) healing, as it is often called. Particularly those who with contact healing might put up a mental barrier and by the negative (repelling) vibration they instil within their aura, neutralise the positive effect that the healing energies can have. But, when distant healing is transmitted, and on a conscious level they are unaware, they do not repel the positive waves of energy.

Psychic or Spiritual Surgery

At times what is termed "psychic surgery" or "spiritual surgery" can be similar to and even utilise spiritual healing, with healing energies being transferred to a recipient. However, it can also go further, and involve surgical procedures. These are often performed while the healer is in a state of trance, when a spirit healer or doctor, as with general trance mediumship, utilises the physical faculties of the medium. Generally, little or no pain is experienced by the 'patient' and recovery is far quicker than with physical surgery.

More often than not no obvious physical instruments are used, although the controlling spirit seems capable of handling spirit equivalents which remain invisible to physical eyesight. Treatments can involve the opening and closing of wounds, although the only physical evidence which might remain is occasional small marks, and these generally fade within a day or two.

Procedures beyond the abilities of current earthly capabilities have been recorded. However, like all forms of healing, no healer or spirit surgeon can guarantee 100% success.

All mediums are wonderful to witness or experience, especially those more accomplished. Unfortunately, as in many walks of life, rogues who seek financial gain also exist. But with an open-minded approach, via a reputable established organisation (see Websites), or one of the many independently run groups, genuine mediumship can be witnessed and experienced.

8. The Spirit and the Aura

This final chapter is included to teach more about the spirit and the aura.

It is not a definitive explanation of how the spirit or soul links with the physical body. Indeed, I am not privy to the full 'mechanics' of this. Hopefully though, it will be sufficient to give an outline and, if so desire, greater understanding can be sought elsewhere.

By the way, our soul is our unique individuality - our essence, whereas spirit is the energy, the power behind and within all life. (The terms are often used to mean the same thing because we are all spirit empowered beings).

As may be gathered, upon Earth we are surrounded and interpenetrated by a mixture of finer structured energies often called the "aura".

It is generally taught that in total the aura - that links with the physical body - consists of seven fields or bodies of spirit energy. Each of them resonating (or vibrating) at their own specific frequency.

Basically, it can be said that the spirit links with the physical body through these finer energy bodies and that each contain chakras, which are energy centres or vortices.

"Chakra" is a word of Sanskrit origin, and signifies a "wheel". These connect through to corresponding physical glands of the physical body; and from these along meridian pathways (which are spirit energy channels) to organs, then onward to nerves, blood, bone, tissue and all parts of the physical body, with not a cell excluded from vibrational connection. The finer energy bodies also relate to levels of consciousness.

When seen clairvoyantly or through aura

photographic techniques (which I do not believe reveal the full extent of the finer energy bodies), they produce an appearance of ever shifting and changing combinations of coloured patterns.

Each finer energy body and chakra has a balance or mid-point to its range, an ideal or optimum frequency, at which rate, if we are in perfect harmony, they will vibrate more distinctly. When, because of some inharmonious thought or action, or because of some external interference, they 'stray' from their ideal frequency, mental, emotional, or physical stability or health can suffer.

The finer energy bodies can also be considered as transformers, in the sense that they are each capable of receiving and recording vibrational 'messages' or 'signals', and where appropriate, relaying or transmitting the information.

They process all information, thoughts, feelings, impressions, and actions at all levels, physical, emotional, mental and spiritual. They are in effect receiving, transforming and sending 'stations' of immense sophistication, capable of evaluating every scrap of information received.

The finer energy bodies are composed of increasing, or progressively finer or subtler forms of ethereal (or sub-atomic) matter, as they extend outwards. It might therefore (and quite correctly) be concluded that we *are* energy beings, temporarily connected and functioning through a physical body, which itself is a form of energy.

The following list includes something about each of the seven finer energy bodies. I have chosen to use what I consider the most appropriate names to describe them although, in some teachings, a number of other names are at times used. While the order and finer detail is also described a little differently in some teachings.

My descriptions are what I have loosely accepted as accurate.

However, I would suggest that it is unnecessary to get too 'hung-up' or over-concerned by names, sequences, or even the exact purposes and the like of each of these finer energy bodies. It is how we live upon Earth that matters! Not how we name and detail things of the spirit. So please simply considered the details I include as a guide only.

1. Elemental - The elemental body is the closest to the physical body, which also has its own electromagnetic counterpart. It is said to link with the base chakra, located at the base of the spine, and with the adrenal glands, and along the meridian pathways with the kidneys, colon, spinal column, bones and legs.

It is the grounding body that draws or connects us to Earth, as a cohesive bonding link it enables the spirit to bind to the physical, while it also attempts to balance our earthly elements. To maintain a healthy state at this level of being it is every person's responsibility to care for his or her own physical body. To where possible, have an adequate and healthy diet, and to take a reasonable amount of exercise.

As can be gathered, and I am sure appreciated, a healthy balance is not necessarily easy to achieve or maintain; rest and activity in moderation are required, along with harmony in all actions. If this level of the aura is seen clairvoyantly, in a healthy condition, it will appear predominantly clear bright blood red.

2. Vital - The vital body is said to link with the spleen chakra, located in the proximity of the spleen near the navel and with the gonad glands, and along the meridian pathways with the womb, ovaries, testicles, bladder, spleen, and nervous system.

This body is the container of the vital energy received physically from the sun, and superphysically from the ever-flowing spiritual reservoirs of life-force energy. It is called the vital body because it is the one that gives vitality to the physical.

The vital body oversees every atom and cell of the physical body, and recognises every imbalance and deficiency, and attempts to keep the balance correct. If necessary, because a deficiency is insurmountable, it will choose to keep one aspect going, such as a vital organ, to the detriment of other aspects.

Breakdowns in health are unavoidable when vital

energy sustaining substances are too depleted. If seen clairvoyantly, in a healthy condition, it will appear predominantly clear bright orange.

3. Astral - The astral body is said to link with the solar plexus chakra, located at the base of the sternum and with the pancreas gland, and along the meridian pathways with the stomach, liver, gallbladder, pancreas and nervous system.

This is the body of desire, often called the emotional body. If desire is too strong this body will appear coarser with colours less than beautiful. When we recognise the reality of spiritual life and our purpose for incarnation, and align this with our emotional desires and reactions, the astral body grows finer with colours more beautiful. The colours can change rapidly, as emotional changes occur.

At the onset of a shock or trauma the astral body shrinks, as does the solar plexus chakra, causing the glands and organs it links with to likewise shrink, or to become restricted. If this is very severe it can block the flow of energy along the meridian pathways, and cause physical damage, as the tissue is constricted and cannot move or function properly.

Under such circumstances, those with the ability to see the aura would see a smaller or contracted aura, as well as one with murkier or darker colours. To keep the astral body in balance it needs calmness and tranquillity, allowing it to perceive clearly.

If seen in a healthy condition, the astral body appears predominantly as a glowing yellow, and when reaching towards the next level of consciousness, would take on a brilliant golden yellow, indicating clarity in the emotions.

4. Etheric (Or, Lower Mind) - The etheric body is said to link with the heart chakra, located over the heart, and with the thymus gland, the immune system, and along the meridian pathways with the heart, lungs, circulatory system, arms and hands.

This is the body of more 'down to Earth' thought. It should be more dominant than the astral body; to be the controlling body of Earth-will although, sometimes, the astral body can reverse this role, causing one to become extremely sensitive, highly volatile, easily upset, irrational and undisciplined.

The etheric body is responsive to all that is happening throughout the other lower bodies and, provided the astral is not allowed dominance, will direct operations, stimulating conscious thought with creative ideas and awareness.

To keep it in balance, it needs reason to be brought to bear, and calm thinking, which will also help the other bodies. The effects of stress, worry or fear can cause this body and the heart chakra to shrink, and the flow of energy along the meridian pathways to become restricted or blocked, causing physical constriction first to the thymus gland, then to the heart and lungs.

The etheric body embraces imagination and dreams. While if this is transformed towards higher aspirations, it can develop the potential for clairvoyance, and greater determination and will.

If the etheric body is seen in a healthy condition, it appears predominantly bright green, and when it is seen as bright emerald green, this indicates stability and power.

5. Mental (Or, Higher Mind) - The mental body is said to link with the throat chakra, located over the throat, and with the thyroid gland, and along the meridian pathways with the lungs, throat and mouth.

This body is at the level of abstract or creative mind, free from the self-imposed restrictions of the ego. It absorbs and stores the knowledge we gain from the myriad of experiences and lessons of our lower bodies.

The directional influence of the mental descends into the etheric level of consciousness through the intuition or conscience, giving inspiration, discipline, planning, and humility with power, love and balance. When seen the colour of the mental body appears predominantly azure (sky) blue.

6. Spiritual - The spiritual body is said to link with the brow chakra, located over the forehead, and with the pituitary gland, and along the meridian pathways with the left eye, ears, nose, the nervous system and the lower part of the brain.

This is the body or level of consciousness of spirit intellect and intuitiveness, of true spiritual knowledge, truth and wisdom.

A greater oneness with all life and a greater perception of reality is understood at this level. It is the level of consciousness to which it is said the Buddha, and many others throughout history, had reached, and in consequence were considered divine messengers of God.

The spiritual body, if it is seen, appears predominantly indigo (dark blue).

7. Celestial - The celestial body is said to link with the crown chakra, located over the crown of the head, and with the pineal gland, and along the meridian pathways with the right eye, the higher part of the brain, and the nervous system.

This body is by many, particularly in Indian teachings, said to be the body of 'ultimate' spiritual attainment. Having the ability to access and merge with levels of higher thought (the higher mind), and thus form a link with all previous knowledge and with still higher levels of consciousness.

From this level we can, if we so wish, move-on to expand our awareness on pathways at present undreamed of, and perhaps currently beyond our comprehension.

The celestial body, if glimpsed, appears predominantly violet to purple.

These are the seven bodies, or levels of consciousness, which are said to be in use while we are in physical form. They are also the bodies we use as we progress through the spiritual realms.

In addition to being the finer energy bodies' link to the physical body, the chakras and meridians are centres and pathways for the flow of life-force energy. The base chakra draws strength from the Earth's energies to give us basic physical strength, while the other chakras draw more refined and progressively higher vibrational spiritual or super-physical energy from the atmosphere.

This energy is vital to our wellbeing, it flows into and

stimulates the physical body via the glands, and it is when the flow of this life-force energy is restricted that we are more likely to become ill.

When the chakras are in a healthy condition they have (clairvoyantly) been seen to spin or pulsate at great speed, the base chakra being the slowest, and they become progressively faster upwards to the crown.

When the chakras spin at their ideal rates we are generally healthy and full of life and vigour.

I think what knowledge of the aura, these finer energy bodies, effectively teach us is that:

We, all spirit life, and this includes us on Earth, is far greater, grander and more interesting and complex than mere labels and any descriptions that we can ever hope to give, and to truly understand in its totality, in our limited earthly language.

The following points are a summary that I have included in a couple of my books, such as, *The Reason Why You Were Born*. Please feel free to share these points with friends and family. I call these:

The Spirit Facts of Life

1. We are all eternal "Souls" (or spirits) experiencing through physical bodies.

2. Higher levels of eternal life do exist, often called the "spirit world", and this world is our natural home when discarnate (not on Earth).

3. Souls from the spirit world can communicate with people incarnate on Earth, and influence and guide them in their lives. Although we always have freewill, so whether we respond to any guidance (that comes to us through our intuition or conscience) is our own decision to make.

4. We generally agree or accept an incarnation life-plan before birth.

5. The Soul undertakes many physical lifetimes (also known as "reincarnation") in order to progress. These present the Soul with the opportunity to encounter many different situations, some difficult or challenging and those more enjoyable.

As we learn from these experiences we naturally increase the vibrations of our soul energies, and this enables us (the Soul) to progress to higher levels of spirit expression. Some of these incarnations could have been on other planets.

6. Whilst on Earth (as in the spirit realms) our soul is subject to universal laws that will eventually fulfil or outwork themselves.

7. The Power which many people call God or the Great Spirit manifests in many ways (the whole of creation is a manifestation). Humans are individualised aspects of this eternal Power.

8. Other life forms also exist at higher rates of spirit vibration and expression, including those called "Angelic".

9. The soul progresses (or evolves) gradually through eternity. Initial and early progress is made via the group stages of expression. Then to the individualised level of expression which human souls have reached.

This highlights the interconnectedness and interdependency of all life, including the world of nature – the plants and trees, insects, birds, fish etc., and the animal kingdom. When we deliberately, thoughtlessly or selfishly destroy any of these, we bring upon ourselves the karmic consequences of our actions.

Conclusion

What empowers physical form, giving it consciousness, mind and personality, thoughts and feelings is pure eternal-indestructible energy known as "spirit".

When the physical form reaches a condition where it becomes untenable for the spirit (known as the "soul" in its individualised state) to continue empowering it, it departs, like the Butterfly leaving the chrysalises.

These facts are true for every single person who has or ever will live upon this planet (or elsewhere).

Whether "in spirit" or presently experiencing through a physical form we are in essence eternal energy beings. We are capable of blending our energies, spirit to spirit, to facilitate mind-to-mind contact to communicate with each other.

As may be appreciated – this is more natural and easy to do when both souls are in the spirit realms and on the same level of consciousness and frequency. However, even when one is in spirit and one on Earth it is still possible to blend energies and transmit images, thoughts and feelings to each other.

This is exactly what transpires with mediums on Earth. A spirit person draws close to them and establishes communication. This is more possible with a medium because their vibrations are suitably 'sympathetic' to such a link, and more so than the average person. As a result they are able to consciously recognise communications and relay these to other people.

The communications arrive via the aura of a medium, which in essence is part of their spirit.

These communications are natural because we are all spirit beings. Lifetimes on Earth are experiences we have chosen to learn through. We are like actors upon the stage of life, playing different roles.

The productions we take part in are the "ultimate" in terms of believability because we, generally, arrive with no memories of spirit life and past physical lifetimes experienced by the soul. This enables us to start afresh, free from past conditions which could disrupt responses appertaining to the current lifetime.

Past memories do however remain within us, because nothing can be totally expunged from our own higher consciousness. This is why hypnosis can open the door to memories of spirit life and past physical lives. As can meditation, dreams and near-death experiences. While some people do manage to carry certain recollections into their present lifetime; which is why young children sometimes remember past experiences on Earth.

Other than clairvoyantly or through materialisation, spirit people or animals are invisible to those of us upon Earth because their rate of vibration is faster than the speed of light and therefore beyond the optical range of our physical eyes. Yet they are there - around us and with us on many occasions, as their communications prove.

Communication is not straightforward or easy. It requires a medium, whether mental, trance, physical, or artistic.

Naturally, we should "test the spirits" and the

mediums, and not take everything they may say without consideration and deliberation. However, we should do so with an open mind and this will undoubtedly prove to us all that life is eternal, and that genuine mediums are able, to varying degrees of accuracy, to communicate with those residing in the spiritual realms.

I trust that I have included within this book sufficient information to help readers to understand how psychics and mediums work, and more about the aura and the spirit nature of life.

This book is short and 'to the point' and I believe very reasonably priced. Hopefully this will encourage readers to recommend it to their friends and family because, it is by helping to enlighten others that *we* can all make a difference in this world.

This can also help to raise awareness and consciousness upon this planet, so that sooner, rather than later, it may become a nicer place for future generations to incarnate.

Perhaps we should also bear in mind the fact that it may of course be *ourselves* returning to be one of a future generation!

So we may also be helping our future self!

Websites

Spiritist & Spiritualist

www.snu.org.uk – The Spiritualists' National Union

www.sagb.org.uk – Spiritualist Association of Great Britain

http://bussuk.webs.com – British Union of Spiritist Societies

www.ism.org.uk – The Institute of Spiritualist Mediums

www.greaterworld.net – Christian Spiritualists

www.whiteagle.org – White Eagle

www.spiritualistresources.com

www.silverbirchpublishing.co.uk – Silver Birch books

Spiritual Healing

www.harryedwardshealingsanctuary.org.uk

www.thehealingtrust.org.uk – Nat. Fed. Of Spiritual Healers

https://ministrymoe.org - Stephen Turoff, Healer-Surgeon

http://raybrownhealing.com – Healer-Surgeon

www.spiritsurgeon.co.uk – Ed Pearson

Trance Mediums

www.kevinryerson.com – Kevin Ryerson

www.suzannegiesemann.com - Suzanne Giesemann

www.whitefeatherspirit.com – Robert Goodwin

Physical Mediums

www.scottmilligan.net

Spiritual Mediums-Artists

www.raye-edwina-brown.com

www.sandyingham.co.uk

NDE Links

https://iands.org – Int. Association for Near-death Studies

www.anitamoorjani.com – Anita Moorjani

http://ebenalexander.com – Eben Alexander

Magazines

http://psychicnews.org.uk

Animal Communicators

www.ameliakinkade.com

www.animalspirit.org - Anna Breytenbach

Spirit Voice Recordings

www.leslieflint.com

Other Informative Links

www.iisis.net – Reincarnation Research

www.spr.ac.uk – Society for Psychical Research

www.windbridge.org – Studying dying, death and what next

www.sheldrake.org – Science and Spiritual

www.lucistrust.org – Alice Bailey books etc.

www.victorzammit.com – Scientific Evidence

Recommended Reading

My Top Recommendation

Victor & Wendy Zammit - *A Lawyer Presents the Evidence for the Afterlife*

Some of My Personal Favourites

Allan Kardec - *The Spirit's Book*

Brian Sadler - *The Meaning and Purpose of Life*

Irene Sowter - *Tails to Tell - The Extraordinary Experiences of an Animal Healer*

Kevin Ryerson and Stephanie Harolde - *Spirit Communication-The Soul's Path*

Robert & Amanda Goodwin - Three titles (from many) - *In the Presence of White Feather - The Enlightened Soul – The Collected Wisdom of White Feather*

Other Highly Recommended

Alice Bailey - *The Consciousness of the Atom*

Anita Moorjani – Dying to be Me - My journey from cancer, to near-death, to true healing

Anthony Borgia - Three books (from many) - *Life in the World Unseen* - *More about Life in the World Unseen* - *Here and Hereafter*

Arthur Findlay – Two titles (from many) - *The Rock of Truth* – *The Curse of Ignorance*

Carol Bowman - *Return from Heaven* (Reincarnation within the same family)

Eben Alexander - *Proof of Heaven* (NDE experience)

Emma Hardinge Britten – *The Faiths, Facts and Frauds of Religious History*

Felicity Joan Medland - *Life around My Father Harry Edwards*

Frederick C. Sculthorp - *Excursions to the Spirit World* (Astral Projection)

Gary E. Schwartz Ph.D. - *The Afterlife Experiments - Breakthrough Scientific Evidence of Life after Death*

Ivy Northage - Two titles: *Journey Beyond* (Trance talks by Chan); *Spiritual Realisation* (Communicated by Chan)

Lynne McTaggart - *The Field* (Scientific investigations)

Michael Newton - Two titles - *Journey of Souls* - *Destiny of Souls*

Paul Miller - *Faces of the Living Dead* (The amazing psychic art of Frank Leah)

Penny Sartori (Dr) – *The Wisdom of Near-Death Experiences*

Ramus Branch - *Harry Edwards - The life story of the great healer*

Raymond Smith - Sir Oliver Lodge spirit group (one of three) - *The Truth the Whole Truth and Nothing but the Truth*

Robin P. Foy - *In Pursuit of Physical Mediumship*

Silver Birch - Three titles (from many) - *Silver Birch Anthology - The Seed of Truth - Light from Silver Birch*

Stephen Turoff - *Seven Steps to Eternity*

Ursula Roberts - Two titles: *Wisdom of Ramadahn - More Wisdom of Ramadahn*

White Eagle – Two titles (from many) - *Walking with the Angels - Spiritual Unfoldment 2*

About the Author

James McQuitty was born in Putney, London in 1950, and worked there for many years before moving to Ryde, Isle of Wight, UK in 1992.

He began to seriously study spiritual philosophy in 1981, and at this time he also began to regularly attend demonstrations by the renowned medium *Jessie Nason*.

Since then he has had many personal experiences and seen spirit visitors on numerous occasions, as well as receiving a great number of spirit communications via other mediums. These include a trance communication message that led to him becoming an author, with the release of his first book in 1994.

In his books he shares an understanding of our true status in this universe, which is that of immortal souls, and much, much more.

His writing style is easy to read and understand, enabling even those who are new to the subjects covered to finish highly informed and greatly inspired.

Printed in Great Britain
by Amazon